P9-CRB-403

Catholic Saints Prayer Book

Moments of Inspiration from Your Favorite Saints

Donna-Marie Cooper O'Boyle

Our Sunday Visitor Publishing Division
Our Sunday Visitor, Inc.
Huntington, Indiana 46750

Nihil Obstat:
Rev. Michael Heintz
Censor Librorum

Imprimatur:
✠ John M. D'Arcy
Bishop of Fort Wayne-South Bend
December 20, 2007

The *Nihil Obstat* and *Imprimatur* are declarations that a work is free from doctrinal or moral error. It is not implied that those who have granted the *Nihil Obstat* and *Imprimatur* agree with the contents, opinions, or statements expressed.

Our Sunday Visitor Publishing Division
Our Sunday Visitor, Inc.
200 Noll Plaza
Huntington, IN 46750

ISBN: 978-1-59276-285-9 (Inventory No. T374)
LCCN: 2007942825

Cover design: Amanda Miller
Cover art: Shutterstock
Interior design: Sherri L. Hoffman
Interior art: Margaret Bunson

PRINTED IN CHINA

Table of Contents

Dedicated with great love …

To my five children: Justin, Chaldea, Jessica, Joseph, and Mary-Catherine.

Acknowledgments

I am most grateful to Jacquelyn Lindsey at Our Sunday Visitor for having faith in me to go forward with this book. I'd like to also thank the entire team at Our Sunday Visitor.

As always, I am thankful to my parents and my family: my mother, Alexandra Mary Uzwiak Cooper, and my father, Eugene Joseph Cooper, in loving memory and thanksgiving for bringing me into this world. Also, my thanks to the blessing of my brothers and sisters: Alice Jean, Gene, Gary, Barbara, Tim, Michael, and David. And to my husband, David, for his loving support.

Introduction

What can the saints of yesterday offer us today? Transcending history, they offer us timeless wisdom and inspiration, while bringing us closer to God. Sanctity surpasses time and is forever near us.

The saints' exemplary examples of holiness give us unparalleled help and sustain our hope, especially during trying times. Just as our association with fellow Christians helps us come closer to Jesus, so our communion with the saints in heaven helps join us to Jesus, but more perfectly.

The *Catechism of the Catholic Church* tells us, "We can and should ask [the saints] to intercede for us and for the whole world" (CCC 2683). Saints are invoked for both the most pressing and the most trivial of needs.

The Church recognizes the saints, who have preceded us into heaven, as holy individuals sharing in the living tradition of prayer. The saints have contemplated God and praised and honored Him by their lives of heroic virtue.

When the Church canonizes the saints, it solemnly proclaims that they lived in fidelity to God's grace and the Church's teachings and have practiced heroic virtues. This formal process of canonization was first put into place by Pope Urban VIII in 1634.

Each year, on November 1, we honor all of the saints in heaven, both canonized and uncanonized. Pope John Paul II told us to pray for more saints and that "more than reformers the Church has a need for saints, because saints are the authentic and most fruitful reformers."

Saints are people from differing walks of life and eras, races, and temperaments. But they are alike in that they all possessed an absolute faith in God and His promises. They all *chose* to become holy people, keeping the Ten Commandments, loving God and their neighbor with all their hearts, souls, and minds. They were united in love — love for God and mankind. Because they were open to God's holy will in their lives, God used them as His instruments to further His kingdom.

We can see the wisdom and holiness of the saints through the conduct of their lives. It shines through the ways they have loved and in their faithfulness to their state in life. Many times their lives were given in service to the very least of God's children or the poorest of the poor.

Ultimately, we should see the saints as models of sanctity for us to imitate, as well as tremendous intercessors, helping us when we invoke them. We should indeed seek out the saints, who will surely help lead us to God, assisting us all along the way.

The saints realized that their work for the Lord would not stop at their death but would continue into eternity. St. Dominic reassured his brothers as he was dying: "Do not weep, for I shall be more useful to you after my death, and I shall help you then more effectively than during my life." St. Thérèse of Lisieux said, "I want to spend my heaven doing good on earth."

Let us invoke the saints often, asking for their holy assistance, even praying along with them, striving to imitate their virtues while praying to become saints ourselves. In doing so, we hope not just to make it to heaven one day, but rather to bring countless souls with us because of our life and how we have loved.

CHRIST AND THE APOSTLES

*"The Church of God needs saints today.
This imposes a great responsibility on us.
We must become holy, not because we want
to feel holy, but because Christ must
be able to live his life fully in us."*

— BLESSED TERESA OF CALCUTTA

1. St. Anne

First century B.C. • Feast Day: July 26

Patroness of homemakers, widows, childless women, pregnant women, nursemaids, lace makers, broom makers, horsemen, grandparents, plague victims

> *"Through the centuries the Church has become ever more aware that Mary, 'full of grace' through God (Lk 1:28), was redeemed from the moment of her conception."* — CATECHISM OF THE CATHOLIC CHURCH (CCC 491)

According to ancient tradition, St. Anne and St. Joachim, her husband, were both from the tribe of Judah, of the royal house of David. They are venerated by the Church as the parents of the Blessed Virgin Mary. St. Anne has been honored as a saint from early Christian times. She and her husband waited patiently for God to grant them a child, and their wait was rewarded with a holy child — the Blessed Mother Mary.

Numerous churches, cathedrals, and hospitals have been dedicated in Anne's honor. She is often represented as teaching her daughter, Mary, the Scriptures. She is invoked by expectant women and mothers everywhere for her intercession because she was privileged to receive such graces and worthy to be the mother of the Mother of God.

Dear St. Anne, beautiful grandmother of Jesus, mother of the Blessed Mother, please pray for me to deepen my prayer life and love for God. Ask God to grant me the graces that I need most. Please show me the way to your daughter, Mary, who will indeed lead me to Jesus. St. Anne, pray for us and for all who invoke your aid. If it is in God's holy will, please grant me (here mention your request). Amen.

2. St. Anthony of Padua

1195-1231 · Feast Day: June 13

Doctor of the Church; patron of Native Americans, the poor, amputees, the elderly, expectant mothers, fishermen, mariners, oppressed people, seekers of lost articles, travelers, domestic animals, harvests; against shipwrecks, starvation, sterility

> *"Actions speak louder than words; let your words teach and your actions speak. We are full of words but empty of actions, and therefore are cursed by the Lord, since he himself cursed the fig tree when he found no fruit but only leaves. It is useless for a man to flaunt his knowledge of the law if he undermines its teaching by his actions."*
> — ST. ANTHONY OF PADUA

*F*erdinand de Bulhoes was born into a wealthy family in Lisbon, Portugal, in 1195. He was the son of a knight, and his family wanted him to be a great nobleman. He wanted to serve God as a priest. Ferdinand joined the Canons Regular of St. Augustine when he was 15. He was ordained in 1219 or 1220.

The bodies of St. Berard and his companions, the first Franciscan martyrs, were brought to Ferdinand's church to be buried. Ferdinand then became inspired to join the Franciscan Friars Minor, taking the name Anthony. He traveled to Morocco to evangelize the Muslim Moors, but illness forced his return to Assisi.

One day a scheduled speaker could not make it to an ordination, so the brothers pressed Anthony to speak instead. His impromptu sermon was impressive, and so began his public career. He traveled throughout Italy and France, preaching and teaching theology. He became well known for his eloquent and persuasive sermons, which drew huge crowds. Anthony was extremely successful in converting countless souls, by God's grace, through his preaching and in his role as a confessor.

The friar settled in Padua in 1226 and completely reformed the city through his preaching. He worked tirelessly for the

ST. ANTHONY OF PADUA

13

poor and for the conversion of heretics. Anthony traveled to Camposanpiero for a brief respite from illness and exhaustion, but he died on the way back to Padua.

Anthony was thirty-six when he died on June 13, 1231. He was canonized the following year, and Pope Pius XII declared him a Doctor of the Church in 1946.

Anthony was without doubt one of the greatest preachers of all time. He was nicknamed "Hammer of the Heretics" and "Living Ark of the Covenant" by his associates. A visitor once reported seeing him with the Infant Jesus held on his arm, a scene often depicted in art. Today he is known as the "Wonder Worker" because of the countless miracles attributed to his intercession, and he is widely invoked for the return of lost articles.

Prayer to St. Anthony of Padua

Dear St. Anthony, you lived your life proclaiming the gospel, not only in word but in action. Your zeal to convert souls brought you to the point of exhaustion. Help me to learn from you so that I may place the things of God above everything else. Your life of holiness was so evident that you were canonized only a year after your death. Help me to strive for holiness always. St. Anthony, pray for us and for all who invoke your aid. If it is in God's holy will, please grant me (here mention your request). Amen.

3. St. Augustine

354-430 • Feast Day: August 28

Patron of brewers, theologians, printers, those who suffer with sore eyes

"This is the business of our life: by labor and prayer to advance in the grace of God, till we come to that height of perfection in which, with clean hearts, we may behold God." — St. Augustine

St. Augustine was born on November 13, 354, in North Africa. Augustine's father was a pagan who converted on his deathbed. His mother was St. Monica, a very devout Christian.

Augustine lost his faith as a young child and lived a worldly life. He lived with a woman from the age of fifteen to thirty. He had a son with her named Adeodatus (meaning "gift from God"). Augustine joined the Manichaean cult. St. Monica prayed intensely for his conversion, and her prayers were eventually answered. Augustine left the cult. He was baptized by St. Ambrose of Milan.

After his mother's death, Augustine returned to Africa, giving the proceeds of his property to the poor and founding a monastery. A monk, a priest, and a theologian, he became the bishop of Hippo, a city in North Africa, in 396. He founded religious communities and fought against the heresies of Manichaeism,

Pelagianism, and Donatism. He was later declared a Doctor of the Church.

Augustine beautifully expressed the human condition when he said: "Our hearts were made for you, O Lord, and they are restless until they rest in you." He wrote many prayers, among them this famous one:

Breathe in me, O Holy Spirit, that my thoughts may all be holy. Act in me, O Holy Spirit, that my work, too, may be holy. Draw my heart, O Holy Spirit, that I may love only what is holy. Strengthen me, O Holy Spirit, to defend all that is holy. Guard me, then, O Holy Spirit, that I always may be holy. Amen.

Augustine died August 28, 430, at Hippo.

Prayer to St. Augustine

Dear St. Augustine, you said, "Access is possible: Christ is the door. It was opened for you when his side was opened by the lance. . . . Your purification is in that water, your redemption is in that blood." Help me, please, to find the door in Christ. Teach me to be steadfast in prayer as you learned from the example of your mother. Help me to steer away from things that are not of God, distractions from the world and deceptive philosophies that offer a supposedly easier way. Please pray for me to have the grace never to turn my back on God. St. Augustine, pray for us and for all who invoke your aid. If it is in God's holy will, please grant me (here mention your request). Amen.

4. St. Benedict

480-543 · Feast Day: July 11

Patron of Europe and against poisoning

"To pray for one's enemies in the love of Christ; to make peace with one's adversary before sundown and never to despair of God's mercy."
— ST. BENEDICT

St. Benedict was born in the year 480 at Nursia, in southern Italy, to a noble Roman family. Benedict saw the corruption of the world in his youth and left home to live in a cave in the mountain of Subiaco, near Rome. There he was taught the Christian ascetical life by St. Romanus.

Benedict quickly attracted a large number of disciples because of his holiness. In 529, he left for Monte Cassino, where he founded the great abbey that became a center of the religious life in Europe.

Abbot Benedict wrote "The Rule," instructions for monastic life that would become the basis of religious life for all Western religious orders and congregations of his time. The Rule teaches the way to perfection through mortification, humility, obedience, prayer, silence, and detachment from the world. Some conspired against him, not wanting to obey the Rule. However, countless souls were converted by Benedict's holiness and his Rule of life.

Many miracles have been attributed to Benedict, including raising a boy from the dead. He trusted God for everything. Money and food always showed up when he needed it.

Benedict foretold the day of his death and was then seized with a violent fever.

ST. BENEDICT

On the sixth day of illness, March 21, 543, he was carried into the chapel by his disciples to receive the Body and Blood of Jesus. He then raised his arms to heaven and prayed his last prayer before dying at the altar. Many miracles have occurred through Benedict's intercession.

The highly esteemed medal of St. Benedict dates back to the time of the abbot himself, who frequently battled evil spirits. The St. Benedict medal is blessed with three solemn prayers by a Benedictine monk or authorized priest; one of the blessings is an exorcism. This medal is known for having much power over evil. It offers powerful protection in spiritual and temporal needs when worn or used with devotion and a trust in the life-giving power of the Holy Cross and the merits of St. Benedict.

Prayer to St. Benedict

Dear St. Benedict, so many miracles have been attributed to you. Your reputation to protect against evil is comforting to me as I invoke your assistance. Please protect me, my family, and my loved ones from every evil and all harm. St. Benedict, pray for us and for all who invoke your aid. If it is in God's holy will, please grant me (here mention your request). Amen.

5. St. Bernadette

**1844-1879 • Feast Day: April 16
(February 18 in France)**

Patroness of the sick, shepherds, Christians ridiculed for their piety

"The more I am crucified, the more I rejoice."
— ST. BERNADETTE

Marie Bernarde Soubirous was born at Lourdes, France, on January 7, 1844. As a child she was called Bernadette. She lived in bleak poverty with her family, being uneducated and suffering from asthma.

On February 11, 1858, Bernadette went out to collect firewood on the banks of the Gave River near Lourdes. There, in a cave above the riverbank, the young girl was granted a vision of a beautiful lady who eventually identified herself as the Blessed Virgin Mary.

When Bernadette revealed the vision to others, they responded with severe skepticism and jealousy. Bernadette received additional daily visions from February 18 through March 4, which drew curious crowds once the word got out. The civil authorities were hostile toward Bernadette and tried to frighten her into recanting her story.

Bernadette persisted in her claims. On February 25, a spring began to flow at the cave where there was previously none, and the water proved to be miraculous, capable of healing the sick. In the vision on March 25, the beautiful woman said to Bernadette, "I am the Immaculate Conception."

Our Lady directed the girl to have a chapel built on the site. Many authorities tried to shut down the spring and prevent the construction of the chapel. But the influence and fame of the visions eventually reached Empress Eugenie of France, wife of Napoleon III, who made sure that construction went forward.

In 1866, Bernadette was sent to the Sisters of Notre Dame in Nevers, where she became a sister of the community. She was treated harshly by the mistress of novices. Eventually, it was discovered that Bernadette suffered from a painful, incurable illness, and she died April 16, 1879.

Lourdes has become one of the major pilgrimage destinations of the world. The spring continues to produce miracles, as well as over 27,000 gallons of water each week. After investigation, the apparitions were approved by the Church. Bernadette was beatified in 1925 and canonized in 1933.

Prayer to St. Bernadette

Dear St. Bernadette, how I would have loved to be with you during your privileged times with the Blessed Mother! Your unwavering faith, trust, and humility are an awesome inspiration for us all. Please pray for me to the Blessed Mother for the graces that I need most. Pray that I can have an increase in faith to do the things that God calls me to do, no matter how contrary they may seem to the world. Remind me to pray for the conversion of sinners, as you were called to do. St. Bernadette, pray for us and for all who invoke your aid. If it is in God's holy will, please grant me (here mention your request). Amen.

6. St. Bridget of Ireland

453-523 • Feast Day: February 1

Patroness of newborns, blacksmiths, sailors, midwives, nuns, dairy workers, poultry farmers, poets, fugitives, printers, scholars, children of unmarried parents

"Lord, clothe me with the robes of innocence."
— IRISH BLESSING

St. Bridget was a contemporary of St. Patrick. Very holy, even as a little girl, she loved the poor and often brought them food or clothing. One day she gave the poor her family's pail of milk, and as she went home, she began to fear that her mother would be upset. She prayed, and when she arrived home, her pail was again full of milk!

ST. BRIDGET OF IRELAND

Bridget's father wanted her to marry and felt that she would make a worthy spouse since she was so kind and so pretty. Bridget wanted no part of marriage because she had already given herself entirely to God. She thought that her beauty was responsible for the attention that she received from men, so she prayed that God would take it away. Her prayer was granted, and her father allowed her to enter the convent.

Bridget became the first religious of Ireland and founded a convent. When she was professed a nun, a miracle occurred, and her beauty returned! St. Bridget became known as "Mary of the Irish" because her virtues of gentleness and purity reminded others of the Blessed Mother.

Prayer to St. Bridget of Ireland

Dear St. Bridget, please pray to the Holy Trinity for me for the graces that I need most. Teach me your love for the poor and your total trust in God to work out all things for the good and for His glory. Help me

22

to look beyond the exterior to see the beauty within. Help me to seek only God's perfect will for my life. St. Bridget, pray for us and for all who invoke your aid. If it is in God's holy will, please grant me (here mention your request). Amen.

7. St. Catherine Labouré

1806-1876 • Feast Day: November 28
(formerly December 31)

Patroness of those who practice the Miraculous Medal devotion

> *"God wishes to charge you with a mission. You will be contradicted, but do not fear; you will have the grace. Tell your spiritual director all that passes within you. Times are evil in France and in the world."* — THE BLESSED MOTHER TO ST. CATHERINE, JULY 19, 1830

Catherine was born in France on May 2, 1806. When her older sister, Marie Louise, joined the Sisters of Charity, Catherine took over her jobs within the home, longing to join the sisters one day herself. Catherine was granted a vision of a priest who spoke to her. Later on in life she realized that it was St. Vincent de Paul, the founder of the Daughters of Charity.

After much resistance from her father, the young woman was finally allowed to join the Daughters of

Charity in January 1830, when she was twenty-four. Shortly afterward, Catherine received several extraordinary visions. Some were of St. Vincent and some of Our Lord.

In July of 1830, the Blessed Mother indeed came to Catherine and told her of the great mission that God had for her. Four months later Mary showed Catherine a medal and directed her to have it made. The words, "O Mary, conceived without sin, pray for us who have recourse to thee," were shown to Catherine.

"Have a medal struck upon this model," Our Lady told her. "All those who wear it, when it is blessed, will receive great graces, especially if they wear it around the neck. Those who repeat this prayer with devotion will be in a special manner under the protection of the Mother of God. Graces will be abundantly bestowed upon those who have confidence."

Two years later, the archbishop of Paris declared that the medals were in conformity to the Church's teaching and ordered that two thousand of them be struck. Once these "Medals of the Immaculate Conception" were distributed, miracles, cures, and conversions occurred. Because of these extraordinary graces, the medal became known as the "Miraculous Medal." Over a billion of them had been distributed by the time St. Catherine died on December 31, 1876.

Catherine kept silent about the apparitions, remaining humble until her dying breath. Only her spiritual director and one of her superiors knew about the extraordinary experiences granted to Catherine.

She was beatified in 1933 and canonized July 27, 1947.

Prayer to St. Catherine Labouré

Dear St. Catherine, please pray for me to have the grace to come closer to Our Blessed Mother Mary, who will bring me to her Son, Jesus. Help me to remain humble and to become holy like you. Please ask our dear Blessed Mother to look kindly on me now and shower upon me abundant graces according to the will of God. St. Catherine, pray for us and for all who invoke your aid. If it is in God's holy will, please grant me (here mention your request). Together let us pray, "O Mary, conceived without sin, pray for us who have recourse to thee." Amen.

8. St. Catherine of Siena

1347-1380 • Feast Day: April 29

Patroness of the sick, especially mothers suffering miscarriages; Christians ridiculed for their piety; firefighters, nurses; against fire, sexual temptation

> *"Everything comes from love, all is ordained for the salvation of man, God does nothing without this goal in mind."* — ST. CATHERINE OF SIENA

Catherine was born on March 25, 1347. One afternoon when she was six years old, she went for a walk with her brother. On the way home she saw the Blessed Mother seated upon a throne holding the Christ Child in her arms. The Child looked at Catherine and raised His hand to bless her as He smiled at her. Catherine's heart melted and she lived her whole life afterward wanting to please Jesus so He would smile at her again.

Despite all her prayers, Catherine felt deserted by God until one day she questioned Him. He tenderly reassured her that He had been in her heart the whole time. She was then overwhelmed with peace.

ST. CATHERINE OF SIENA

Soon afterward, Jesus came to Catherine again and told her to care for the poor. He said, "You know that love gives two commandments — to love me and to love your neighbor. I desire that you walk not on one but two feet, and fly to heaven on two wings."

So Catherine began to work with people in need, joining the lay Order of St. Dominic. During the great plague of 1374, Catherine took care of the sick. She had a gift for making everyone around her feel better. In addition, she had the gifts of healing, prophecy, knowledge of the consciences of others, and extraordinary light in spiritual matters. Thousands reformed their lives because of her.

Jesus is said to have presented Catherine with two crowns, one of gold and the other of thorns, asking her to choose between the two. Eagerly taking up the crown of thorns, she forcibly pressed it upon her head. Catherine's love for humiliations and suffering was nurtured by her continuous meditation on the sufferings of Jesus. She also received the sacred stigmata in imitation of the wounds of Christ.

She tirelessly worked to reform the Church and was responsible for Pope Gregory XI's return to Rome from Avignon in 1378, ending the papacy's "exile" in France. Catherine died in Rome on April 29, 1380, at the age of thirty-three. She was canonized in 1461.

Prayer to St. Catherine of Siena

Dear St. Catherine, your remarkable life in service to God and His people is an awesome inspiration to us all. Help me realize that I am to serve Jesus in others, especially the poor and those in need. Please pray to the Blessed Trinity for me to be granted the graces I need to be faithful to God's holy will in my life. St. Catherine, pray for us and for all who invoke your aid. If it is in God's holy will, please grant me (here mention your request). Amen.

9. St. Clare of Assisi

1194-1253 • Feast Day: August 11

Patroness of goldsmiths, laundry workers, embroiderers, those with eye disease; television

> *"Praise and glory to you, O loving Jesus Christ, for the most sacred wound in your side and for your infinite mercy which you have made known to us in the opening of your breast to the soldier Longinus, and so to us all."*
>
> — St. Clare of Assisi

Clare was born in Assisi, Italy, on July 11, 1194, to a noble family. She was so impressed with a sermon from St. Francis in 1212 that she ran away from home, refusing ever to marry. She received the habit from Francis at the Portiuncula chapel.

Clare resisted every effort by her father to have her return home. Later, her fifteen-year-old sister, Agnes, joined her and also received the habit. Their father sent twelve armed men to bring Agnes home. Clare stormed heaven with prayer. As a result, the men found they could not take Agnes away because she became so heavy and could not be budged.

In 1215, Francis made Clare the superior of the newly founded Poor Clares. She led the order for forty years, and during that time her mother and another sister, Beatrice, joined them. The order flourished and spread to other parts of Italy.

Clare and Francis were primarily responsible for the spread of the Franciscan movement. She died on August 12, 1253, and was canonized two years later. Seven centuries later, Pope Pius XII named Clare the patroness of television because one Christmas when Clare was too sick to leave her sickbed, she had a vision in which she saw and heard Midnight Mass from a distance.

Prayer to St. Clare of Assisi

Dear St. Clare, there is so much that I can learn from you. You renounced your wealth so that you could become poor to spend your life serving the poor. You followed the will of God in your life with much strength and zeal, not allowing anything to stand in the way of your dear Lord's plans for you. Please pray that I can have the courage always to follow God's almighty call. St. Clare, pray for us and for all who invoke your aid. If it is in God's holy will, please grant me (here mention your request). Amen.

ST. CLARE OF ASSISI

10. St. Dominic

1170-1221 • Feast Day: August 8

Patron of scientists, especially astronomers; people falsely accused

> *"A man who governs his passions is master of the world. We must either command them, or be enslaved by them. It is better to be a hammer than an anvil."* — St. Dominic

Dominic was born in 1170 in Spain. Dominic's mother had a vision when she was pregnant with him. She saw him as a dog carrying a burning torch to set the world on fire. At his baptism, she saw a star shining from his chest.

Dominic is said to have been ordained while pursuing his studies, receiving the habit of the Regular Canons of St. Augustine. In 1199, he was appointed canon of Osma and then became prior superior of the chapter, which was known for its strict adherence to the rule of St. Benedict.

In 1203, Dominic accompanied Bishop Diego de Avezedo to France, where they preached the gospel with great zeal to the heretics there, who were caught up in the Albigensian heresy. They also helped reform the Cistercian religious order. Dominic then founded a convent of nuns to provide education for children.

Along with six followers, Dominic began to lay out the foundation and rules for his impressive Order of Preachers, called the Dominicans. The order and its rules were approved in 1216.

The last years of Dominic's life were spent traveling around Italy, Spain, and France preaching, organizing the order, setting up new houses, and accumulating members. The Dominicans made great progress in conversion work as they applied Dominic's theory of combining the intellectual life with modern needs. Dominic died in Bologna on August 6, 1221, and was canonized in 1234.

Prayer to St. Dominic

Dear St. Dominic, you stood for truth and worked tirelessly to convert people from error and heresy, opening the gates of heaven for them. Please help me to see that I should not remain idle, but rather work endlessly for the truth and live the gospel. We are told that Blessed Alan de la Roche gave us the gift of the Rosary, which he attributed to you. Help me to realize the great power in praying the Rosary by coming closer to Jesus through His Blessed Mother Mary. St. Dominic, pray for us and for all who invoke your aid. If it is God's holy will, please grant me (here mention your request). Amen.

St. Dominic

11. St. Elizabeth Ann Seton

1774-1821 • Feast Day: January 4

Patroness of the Apostleship of the Sea (her sons worked at sea), children who are dying, families with in-law problems, Christians ridiculed for their piety, those who lose their parents

> *"We know certainly that our God calls us to a holy life. We know that he gives us every grace, every abundant grace; and though we are so weak of ourselves, this grace is able to carry us through every obstacle and difficulty."*
> — ST. ELIZABETH ANN SETON

Elizabeth Ann Bayley's mother died when Elizabeth was three years old. She grew up as an Episcopalian. As a teenager, she read her Bible frequently and came close to God through nature and her church.

In 1794, Elizabeth married William Seton, a man with whom she had fallen deeply in love. She became a magnificent wife and mother. Eventually, though, the family fell into financial ruin, and family members then experienced many sicknesses. Instead of losing her faith, Elizabeth deepened her spirituality through prayer. She cared for her family and also her sick friends.

Elizabeth's husband was stricken with tuberculosis so they went to Italy in search of a cure. They experienced many difficulties in the cold, damp room where they stayed. Will died and Elizabeth and her daughter Ann Marie were quarantined after contracting scarlet fever, preventing their departure. Elizabeth began to understand God's purpose for their detainment in Italy as the truth of the Catholic faith unfolded for her.

Elizabeth was disheartened by the reactions she received from family and friends when she shared her thoughts about the truth of the Catholic faith. Nevertheless, she entered the

St. Elizabeth Ann Seton

Church on March 14, 1805, and went on to found the Sisters of Charity (the first American sisterhood) and the first Catholic parochial school in America. She died January 4, 1821. Elizabeth was beatified March 17, 1963, and canonized on September 14, 1975, the first native-born American to be canonized.

Prayer to St. Elizabeth Ann Seton

Dear St. Elizabeth Ann Seton, please pray for me to be steadfast in prayer. Ask our dear Lord to teach me to seek Him above all things. Help me to be patient with God's holy will in my life so that I may embrace whatever it is that God gives me. St. Elizabeth Ann Seton, pray for us and for all who invoke your aid. If it is in God's holy will, please grant me (here mention your request). Amen.

12. St. Faustina Kowalska

1905-1938 • Feast Day: October 5

Patroness of devotees of the Divine Mercy

> *"Suddenly my spirit was united with God, and in that instant I saw the grandeur and the inconceivable holiness of God and, at the same time, I realized the nothingness I am of myself."*
> — ST. FAUSTINA KOWALSKA

Helena Kowalska was born August 25, 1905. She became a nun in the Congregation of the Sisters of Our Lady of Mercy in Warsaw, Poland, August 1, 1925, after being rejected by several other orders. Her order was dedicated to helping troubled young women.

Having changed her name to Sister Maria Faustina of the Most Blessed Sacrament, the young sister lived in various convents working as cook, porter, and gardener. Faustina had a special devotion to the Blessed Mother, the Blessed Sacrament, and sacramental confession. She developed a deep and mystical interior life, receiving visions and revelations and experiencing a hidden stigmata.

In the 1930s, Faustina received a message from Jesus that she was told to spread around the world — Jesus' message of mercy to each person individually and humanity as a whole. Jesus asked her to have an image of Divine Mercy painted, which portrayed Jesus with the inscription, "Jesus, I trust in You." In

1935, a painting was commissioned that depicted Jesus with red and white light shining from His Sacred Heart. Jesus also asked Faustina to be merciful to everyone.

Faustina recorded her experiences in a diary almost 700 pages long, which was written phonetically because she was nearly illiterate. A bad translation reached Rome and was declared heretical. However, Karol Wojtyla (later Pope John Paul II) ordered a new translation made because he had been inundated by requests for the diary to be reconsidered. Vatican authorities eventually approved the diary, and it was published under the title *Divine Mercy in My Soul.*

In 1996, the Archdiocese of Kraków approved the Apostles of Divine Mercy, a movement of priests, religious, and lay people inspired by the Divine Mercy message given to us by Faustina. It has since spread to twenty-nine countries.

Faustina died from tuberculosis on October 13, 1938, in Kraków, Poland. She was beatified April 18, 1993, and canonized April 30, 2000.

Prayer to St. Faustina Kowalska

Dear St. Faustina, you were privileged to have received the message of Divine Mercy to be spread around the world. You came so intimately close to our dear Lord, Jesus. Please teach me to be merciful always and to put my full trust, with total abandonment, in Jesus. St. Faustina, pray for us and for all who invoke your aid. If it is in God's holy will, please grant me (here mention your request). Jesus, I trust in You! Amen.

13. St. Francis of Assisi

1181-1226 • **Feast Day: October 4**

Patron of families, merchants, lace-makers, ecologists, animals, zoos, Catholic Action

> *"My God and my All!"*
> — ST. FRANCIS OF ASSISI

St. Francis was born in Assisi, in central Italy, in 1181. Francis led a carefree life until he experienced a vision of Christ. As a result, Francis radically changed his life, renouncing luxuries, all earthly possessions and wealth, giving his life fully to the Lord.

Francis went on a pilgrimage to Rome in 1206 and embraced a life of poverty, devoting himself to the care of the poor. Because of this decision, his father disinherited him, considering him a madman.

Francis repaired several churches in Assisi — eventually using the small chapel called the Portiuncula as his headquarters — and then gave himself completely to his life's work of preaching the gospel and practicing holy poverty. Even though Francis never felt worthy enough to be a priest, he attracted many followers. He founded the Franciscans on April 16, 1209, and received verbal approval for the order in 1210 from Pope Innocent III.

At Christmas time in 1223, Francis built a crèche (manger scene) for the people of Grecchio, establishing a custom observed all over the world today. Francis prayed ardently for two gifts from God. First, he wanted to realize in his body and soul the sufferings of Christ. Second, he wanted his heart to be filled, as far as possible, with the same immense love that caused Jesus to undergo extreme sufferings to redeem mankind.

Francis's prayers were profoundly answered in September 1224 when he was observing Lent. He had been meditating on Jesus' passion when a flaming angel in the form of a cross pierced his hands and feet and side with the sacred stigmata — wounds reminiscent of Jesus' wounds on the cross. These remained until his death in 1226.

ST. FRANCIS
OF ASSISI

Prayer to St. Francis of Assisi
Dear St. Francis, you are known as a gentle lover of nature and of the poor. You renounced your wealth and all material things of this world to unite yourself with our wounded Lord to serve His poor. Please, dear St. Francis, pray for me to receive the graces to come closer to Jesus and to discern His holy will in my life. Help me to detach myself from things of this world, so that I may cling only to the things of God. St. Francis, pray for us and for all who invoke your aid. If it is in God's holy will, please grant me (here mention your request). Amen.

14. St. Francis Xavier

1506-1552 · Feast Day: December 3

Patron of all foreign missions, navigators, victims of epidemics

> *"It is not the actual physical exertion that counts towards a man's progress, nor the nature of the task, but the spirit of faith with which it is undertaken."*
> — ST. FRANCIS XAVIER

Francis Xavier was born on April 7, 1506, in the Basque area of Spain, in the family castle of Xavier. Francis met St. Ignatius of Loyola, and along with Ignatius and five others founded the Society of Jesus (the Jesuits) in 1534 at Montmartre, France.

In 1536, Francis met up with Ignatius in Venice, Italy, intending to go on a mission to Palestine, but circumstances prevented the trip from taking place. Francis was ordained in Venice in 1537 and went to Rome in 1538. In 1540, the pope formally recognized the Society and sent Francis with another priest to Lisbon, Portugal, to prepare for becoming the first Jesuit missionaries to the Far East.

Francis traveled on to Goa, India, after a year's voyage. On the way he spent six months in Mozambique, preaching and caring for the sick. In Goa, Francis, along with two other Jesuit priests, preached to the natives, living among them while attempting to reform their fellow Europeans.

Francis converted thousands to the Christian faith over the next decade. In 1542, he visited the tip of India. He also visited the Moluccas (near New Guinea), Morotai (near the Philippines), and Japan. Ignatius appointed Francis the first Jesuit provincial of India and the East. In 1552, Francis set out for China and landed on the island of Sancian. He died before reaching the Chinese mainland.

Francis faced many hardships in his missionary work: resistance from European officials, language barriers, lack of funds, and lack of cooperation. Nevertheless, he persevered, traveling thousands of miles in his bare feet, helping the poor, healing the sick, and raising the dead — all with great zeal and love, leaving his Christian mark wherever he went. Pope Pius X canonized Francis in 1622, proclaiming him patron saint of foreign missions.

Prayer to St. Francis Xavier

Dear St. Francis Xavier, you preached with great zeal without rest, concerned only with furthering God's kingdom and bringing many souls to the Christian faith. Please pray for me that in my own life I may strive to be a missionary, bringing others to the Lord through my life of love and service. St. Francis Xavier, pray for us and for all who invoke your aid. If it is in God's holy will, please grant me (here mention your request). Amen.

15. St. Ignatius of Loyola

1491-1556 · Feast Day: July 31

Patron of retreats and spiritual exercises, the Society of Jesus

> *"If God causes you to suffer much, it is a sign that he has great designs for you, and that he certainly intends to make you a saint. And if you wish to become a great saint, entreat him yourself to give you much opportunity for suffering; for there is no wood better to kindle the fire of holy love than the wood of the cross, which Christ used for his own great sacrifice of boundless charity."*
>
> — ST. IGNATIUS OF LOYOLA

Ignatius was born in 1491 in the family castle of Loyola in Spain. Ignatius entered military service and was wounded in the leg. During his convalescence, he read about the life of Christ and the lives of the saints. He was so impressed that he decided to devote his life to Christ. He went to confession and then spent ten months in solitude at a retreat where he experienced visions and wrote most of his *Spiritual Exercises,* which were published in 1548.

Ignatius next spent ten years studying at universities in Barcelona, Alcala, Salamanca, and Paris. In 1534, he received his Master of Arts degree at age forty-three. He founded the Society of Jesus (the Jesuits) that same year, and in 1537 he and seven of his followers were ordained.

Ignatius had three goals in service to the Church: reform of the Church through education and frequent use of the sacraments; widespread missionary activity; and the fight against heresy. Unable to go on pilgrimage to Jerusalem, Ignatius and his friends journeyed to Rome instead to offer their services to the pope. On the way, he experienced a vision in which Jesus promised that all would be well in Rome. The Society was approved by Pope Paul III in 1540. Ignatius became superior general the following year, and the group took their formal vows.

DEATH MASK OF ST. IGNATIUS OF LOYOLA

At once, Jesuits were sent all over to missionary areas, as far as India in the East and Brazil in the West. Jesuit schools, colleges, and seminaries were founded all over Europe. Ignatius continued to reside in Rome and remained the superior general of the Society for more than fifteen years.

Ignatius died in 1556. He was beatified July 27, 1609, and canonized on March 12, 1622.

Prayer to St. Ignatius of Loyola

Dear St. Ignatius, you fell in love with Christ while recuperating from your war wound. Help me to see that I should consider all that happens to me as opportunities to come closer to the Lord. You worked tirelessly as a missionary to fight heresy and educate people in the faith. Pray for me that I will have your strength and zeal to fight the ever-present heresy in my own culture and to convert souls to spread the kingdom of God. St Ignatius, pray for us and for all who invoke your aid. If it is in God's holy will, please grant me (here mention your request). Amen.

16. St. John Chrysostom

347-407 • Feast Day: September 13

Patron of lecturers, preachers, speakers, victims of epilepsy

> *"If the Lord should give you power to raise the dead, he would give much less than he does when he bestows suffering. By miracles you would make yourself debtor to him, while by your suffering he may become debtor to you. And even if sufferings had no other reward than being able to bear something for that God who loves you, is not this a great reward and a sufficient remuneration? Whoever loves, understands what I say."*
> — ST. JOHN CHRYSOSTOM

John was born around the year 347 at Antioch, in Syria. His father died when he was young, and his mother raised him in holiness. John studied rhetoric under Libanius, a famous orator of that time. The young man embraced an ascetic life and lived in a cave for two years before returning to city life.

Ordained a priest in 386, John proved to be an
eloquent preacher. He spent twelve years ministering

in Syria, where he developed a stomach illness that stayed with him his whole life.

The title "Chrysostom" ("golden-mouthed") was given to John because of his gift of preaching. His sermons would sometimes continue for hours and were always clear and scriptural. In 398, John became archbishop of Constantinople.

John worked to reform the clergy, especially seeking to prevent the sale of Church offices. He fought for the poor and criticized the rich for not sharing their wealth. Working to promote fidelity in marriage, he also encouraged others to be charitable and work for justice. He revised the Greek liturgy and greatly influenced the Church throughout the eastern portion of the empire.

John was removed from his diocese twice by officials because his sermons annoyed nobles and bishops. In 403, he was exiled. He was again banished in 404 and died on the way to his place of exile.

ST. JOHN CHRYSOSTOM

John was declared a Doctor of the Church in 451. His relics are in the choir chapel of St. Peter's in Rome.

Prayer to St. John Chrysostom

Dear St. John Chrysostom, you have said, "God asks little, but he gives much." Please teach me to give much to God. Help me to turn my life over to Him unreservedly. Help me to preach by my word and example so that others may turn to God. St. John Chrysostom, pray for us and for all who invoke your aid. If it is in God's holy will, please grant me (here mention your request). Amen.

17. St. John Neumann

1811-1860 • Feast Day: January 5

First male American citizen and first U.S. bishop to be canonized

> *"A man must always be ready, for death comes when and where God wills it."*
> — ST. JOHN NEUMANN

John Neumann was born in Bohemia (now the Czech Republic) on March 28, 1811. John entered the diocesan seminary of Budweis in 1831. Bohemia had a surplus of priests, so John traveled to the United States in 1836 and was warmly welcomed by Bishop John Dubois of New York because there were only 36 priests there to serve over 200,000 people. John was ordained, and having a choice between working in Buffalo or the rural areas, he chose to live in a log cabin near an unfinished church to serve people in need. Speaking twelve languages fluently, John devoted the next four years to missionary work, ministering to the German-speaking Catholics in upstate

New York. He often lived on bread and water and very little sleep. He walked to all of the remote farms to serve the people, bringing them to God.

When John joined the Redemptorists in 1842, in Pittsburgh, he became the first member of that order to take vows in the United States. His missionary work continued throughout Maryland, Ohio, Pennsylvania, and Virginia. He became rector of St. Philomena's Church in Pittsburgh in 1844 and was named vice regent and superior of the American Redemptorists in 1847.

In 1852, John was consecrated the fourth bishop of Philadelphia. He reorganized the diocese and was an active promoter of Catholic education. He also wrote two catechisms that were endorsed by the American Catholic bishops and were widely used for thirty-five years.

By the time John died on January 5, 1860, in Philadelphia, he had built more than fifty churches, started a cathedral, and established nearly a hundred schools. He was recognized for his great holiness, charity, and preaching. John was beatified on October 13, 1963, and canonized on June 19, 1977.

Prayer to St. John Neumann

Dear St. John Neumann, you always put yourself last and cared for so many around you. Your great love to educate others in the faith should inspire me to do the same. Please pray to the Blessed Trinity for me to be granted the graces that I need most. Help me to be aware of those in my midst who are in need. St. John Neumann, pray for us and for all who invoke your aid. If it is in God's holy will, please grant me (here mention your request). Amen.

18. St. Joseph

First Century • Feast Days: March 19, Joseph the Husband of Mary; May 1, Joseph the Worker

Patron of the Universal Church, fathers, carpenters, the dying, social justice

> *"Joseph, son of David, do not fear to take Mary your wife, for that which is conceived in her is of the Holy Spirit; she will bear a son, and you shall call his name Jesus, for he will save his people from their sins."* — MATTHEW 1:20-21

St. Joseph, foster father of Jesus and husband of Mary, is sometimes referred to as the silent saint. He was humble and holy, "a just man" (Mt 1:19). He was a working man, a carpenter. The angel who greeted Joseph to tell him about Jesus reminds us of Joseph's lineage with the greeting, "son of David," which was a royal title also used for Jesus. Even though Joseph came from royal blood, a descendant from the greatest king of Israel, he was apparently not wealthy. When he and Mary took Jesus to the temple to be circumcised, they offered the humble sacrifice of two turtledoves rather than a lamb — an alternative for those who could not afford a lamb.

Joseph demonstrated great compassion when he learned that his fiancée, Mary, was pregnant, and he knew he was not the biological father. He planned to divorce her quietly so she would not be stoned to death for adultery. Joseph's deep faith gave him the courage to accept Mary as his wife when he learned the truth about Mary's baby from the angel who came to him in his dream.

ST. JOSEPH

Joseph showed his obedience to God when he followed instructions from the angel to flee to Egypt. He followed God's laws for the Jewish people by bringing Mary and Jesus to Jerusalem to have Jesus circumcised and Mary purified after Jesus' birth. We don't know where Joseph was born, but he most likely died before Jesus entered public ministry, because Scripture has no mention of Joseph in its accounts of Jesus' adult life.

The Roman Missal contains this prayer: "Father, you entrusted our Savior to the care of St. Joseph. By the help of his prayers may your Church continue to serve its Lord, Jesus Christ, who lives and reigns with you and the Holy Spirit, one God for ever and ever. Amen."

Prayer to St. Joseph

Dear St. Joseph, you were an ordinary man, a humble carpenter. But you were a prayerful, holy soul, the foster father of Jesus, a model for us all. Please guide me in my own journey through life, and help me be aware of God's specific call to me. Help me to see that in my own life God is calling me to greater things for His glory. Please pray to the Blessed Trinity for me to be granted the graces that I need most. I pray that I can be faithful to my state of life, totally trusting in God's divine providence for me. St. Joseph, pray for all who invoke your aid. If it is in God's holy will, please grant me (here mention your request). Amen.

19. St. Jude Thaddeus

First Century • Feast Day: October 28 (Western Church); June 19 (Eastern Church)

Apostle; patron of desperate, impossible, lost, and forgotten causes; hospitals

> *"But you, beloved, build yourselves up on your most holy faith; pray in the Holy Spirit; keep yourselves in the love of God; wait for the mercy of our Lord Jesus Christ unto eternal life."*
> — JUDE 20-21

Jude was the son of Cleophas and the Mary who stood at the foot of Jesus' cross and anointed His body after the Crucifixion. He was a nephew of the Blessed Mother and Joseph, a blood relative of Jesus.

Ancient tradition says that he looked much like Jesus. Jude's brother was St. James the Lesser. Jude was an apostle and possibly a fisherman.

Jude preached in Syria, Judea, Mesopotamia, Libya, Idumaea, and Persia with St. Simon. He wrote the Letter of Jude, the book immediately preceding Revelation. According to ancient stories he was an exorcist and could cast demons out of pagan idols, causing the demons to flee and statues to fall into pieces.

Jude returned to Jerusalem in the year 62 and assisted in the election of his brother, Simeon, as bishop of Jerusalem. Many early Christians confused Jude with Jesus' betrayer, Judas, so they never prayed for his help. Devotion to St. Jude became a lost cause, and for this reason he acquired the patronage of lost and impossible causes.

Jude was beaten to death (some say shot with arrows) and then beheaded, a martyr for the Christian faith. His relics are at St. Peter's in Rome, at Rheims, and at Toulouse, France.

St. Jude
Thaddeus

Prayer to St. Jude Thaddeus

Dear St. Jude, you stand by God's throne as one of the chosen apostles ready to intercede for us pilgrims here on earth. Please teach me to preach the gospel in my own state of life. You are often invoked as the saint of impossible cases. I come before you now in my necessity imploring your help. Please pray that I may be granted the graces that I need most. St. Jude, pray for us and for all who invoke your aid. If it is in God's holy will, please grant me (here mention your request). Amen.

20. St. Margaret Mary Alacoque

1647–1690 • Feast Day: October 16

Patroness of devotees to the Sacred Heart of Jesus, polio patients, those who lose their parents

> *"What a weakness it is to love Jesus Christ only when he caresses us, and to be cold immediately once he afflicts us. This is not true love. Those who love thus, love themselves too much to love God with all their heart."*
> — ST. MARGARET MARY ALACOQUE

*M*argaret Mary was born on July 22, 1647, in France. When she was eight years old her father died, and Margaret Mary was sent to the Poor Clares school. She became stricken with rheumatic fever and was bedridden until the age of fifteen.

One day Margaret Mary received a vision of the Blessed Mother and was healed of her illness. Later on she received a vision of Jesus after His scourging. She then became inspired to join the Visitation convent at Paray-le-Monial in 1671 and was professed the next year.

From the age of twenty, Margaret Mary experienced visions of Jesus. On December 27, 1673, and for the next year and a half, she received revelations from Jesus. He told her that she was His chosen instrument to spread devotion to His Sacred Heart: "Look at this heart which has loved men so much, and yet men do not want to love me in return. Through you my divine heart wishes to spread its love everywhere on earth."

The twelve promises Jesus told Margaret Mary for those devoted to His Sacred Heart are these:

I will give them all of the graces necessary for their state of life.

I will establish peace in their families.

I will console them in all their troubles.

They shall find in my heart an assured refuge during life and especially at the hour of their death.

I will pour abundant blessings on all their undertakings.

Sinners shall find in my heart the source of an infinite ocean of mercy.

Tepid souls shall become fervent.

Fervent souls shall speedily rise to great perfection.

I will bless the homes where an image of my heart shall be exposed and honored.

I will give to priests the power of touching the
  most hardened hearts.

Those who propagate this devotion shall have
  their names written in my heart, never to be
  effaced.

The all-powerful love of my heart will grant to
  all those who shall receive Communion on
  the first Friday of nine consecutive months
  the grace of final repentance; they shall not
  die under my displeasure, nor without receiving their sacraments; my heart shall be their
  assured refuge at that last hour.

Our Lord instructed the young woman not only
about observance of the Nine First Fridays, but also
the Holy Hour, and He asked that the Feast of the Sacred Heart be established in the Church. Blessed
Claude La Colombiere, the confessor of the community at the time, declared that the visions were gen-
uine.

In 1683, the community observed the Feast of
the Sacred Heart. Two years later a chapel was built
at the Paray-le-Monial in honor of the Sacred Heart.
From there, devotion to the Sacred Heart spread
throughout the Visitation Order.

On October 17, 1690, Margaret Mary died of
natural causes. She was beatified on September 18,
1862, and canonized May 13, 1920. In 1765, sev-
enty-five years after her death, the devotion to the
Sacred Heart of Jesus was officially recognized and
approved by Pope Clement XIII.

Prayer to St. Margaret Mary Alacoque

Dear St. Margaret Mary, you were chosen to be a partaker in the infinite treasures of the Sacred Heart of Jesus. You found every consolation immersed in Jesus' Sacred Heart and professed that Our Lord deserves to be honored and loved at all times. You willingly suffered humiliation and persecution and embraced the Cross to bring Jesus' sacred message to the world. Please teach me how to come close to Jesus' Sacred Heart and intercede for me before His flaming Heart, which burns with love for me, so that I will be granted the graces that I need most. St. Margaret Mary, pray for us and for all who invoke your aid. If it is in God's holy will, please grant me (here mention your request). Most Sacred Heart of Jesus, have mercy on me. Amen.

21. St. Marguerite Bourgeoys

1620-1700 • Feast Day: January 12

Patroness of those who lose their parents, those rejected by religious orders; against poverty and impoverishment

> *"Our Lady's love is like a stream that has its source in the Eternal Fountains, quenches the thirst of all, can never be drained, and ever flows back to its Source."* — ST. MARGUERITE BOURGEOYS

*M*arguerite was born on April 17, 1620. Marguerite's mother died when she was nineteen, leaving Marguerite to care for her younger siblings. When Marguerite was twenty-seven, her father died, and she asked Our Lord what she should do with her life. The governor of Montreal, Canada, was in France at that time, searching for teachers for the New World. He asked Marguerite to come to Canada to teach religion. She accepted the invitation, and in 1653, sailed for Canada.

Upon arriving in Canada, Marguerite helped to build a chapel in honor of Our Lady of Good Help. She also opened her first school in 1658 and returned to France the following year to recruit teachers. She brought four to Canada, and in 1670 returned to France to recruit more teachers, this time coming back with six. These courageous women became the Congregation of Notre Dame.

The sisters reached out to the poor by providing food. They started a vocational school to teach young people the skills to run households and farms. As the congregation grew, Mother Marguerite and her sisters opened several missions, including one for Native Americans.

In 1698, the Church approved Marguerite's religious rule. After that time, Mother Marguerite spent her time in prayer and in writing her autobiography. On December 31, 1699, Mother Marguerite asked Our Lord to take her life instead of a young sister who lay dying. By the following morning, January 1, 1700, the young sister was completely well, and Mother Marguerite was burning up with a fever. She suffered for twelve days and died January 12, 1700. Mother Marguerite was beatified on November 12, 1950, and then canonized on October 31, 1982.

Prayer to St. Marguerite Bourgeoys

Dear St. Marguerite, you lived a life of selflessness and courage, caring for your siblings, giving away your inheritance, and voyaging between two countries to build up your order. Your heart went out to the poor and needy. Please help me to look around and to search my heart as you did to discern where Our Lord wants me to work to help others. Please ask Our Lord and His Blessed Mother to grant me the graces that I need most. St. Marguerite, pray for us and for all who invoke your aid. If it is in God's holy will, please grant me (here mention your request). Amen.

22. St. Maria Goretti

1890-1902 • Feast Day: July 6

Patroness of children, the Children of Mary, those bereaved of parents, martyrs, rape victims, young people; against poverty

"Asked if she forgave her murderer, she replied, 'Yes, for the love of Jesus I forgive him . . . and I want him to be with me in Paradise.'"
— POPE PIUS XII

*M*aria was born October 16, 1890, at Corinaldo, Ancona, Italy. Maria's father died of malaria when she was six, forcing the family to move in order to survive. They went to a farm owned by the man who had been her father's partner.

In 1902, when Maria was only twelve, she was attacked by Alessandro Serenelli, a farmhand who was the son of her father's partner. He tried to rape Maria, who fought back strenuously, screaming to Alessandro that he was committing a sin for which he would go to hell. Alessandro tried to choke Maria into submitting to him and finally stabbed her fourteen times.

Maria died in the hospital two days later, holding a crucifix and a medal of the Blessed Mother. She forgave her attacker and asked God to forgive him.

While Alessandro was in prison for his crime he had a vision of Maria. She smiled at him and offered him a bouquet of lilies. As Alessandro accepted the lilies, they were transformed into white flames. Then Maria disappeared. Because of the vision, Alessandro converted and later testified at Maria's beatification.

Maria was beatified in 1947 and canonized in 1950. The canonization ceremony was attended by 250,000, including her mother. (It is the only time a parent has witnessed her child's canonization.) At the canonization ceremony, Pope Pius XII observed: "Not all of us are expected to die a martyr's death, but we are all called to the pursuit of Christian virtue. So let us all, with God's grace, strive to reach the goal that the example of the virgin martyr, St. Maria Goretti, sets before us."

Prayer to St. Maria Goretti

Dear St. Maria Goretti, you were a brave and holy young woman who knew the importance of preserving your purity for the glory of God. Please help young people everywhere understand the importance of staying close to God so they do not give in to the deceptive allurements of the world. Pray that they have the strength and ability to discern what is of God and what is not, so they one day reach heaven. Dear Maria, your powerful forgiving love converted your attacker's heart and soul. Teach us all to be holy souls and to be forgiving to all. St. Maria Goretti, pray for us and for all who invoke your aid. If it is in God's holy will, please grant me (here mention your request). Amen.

23. St. Maximilian Kolbe

1894-1941 • Feast Day: August 14

Patron of drug addicts, families, journalists, prisoners, especially political prisoners; the pro-life movement

> "[The Blessed Virgin] is a breath of divine power, a most pure effusion of the Most High; hence nothing sullied can ever contaminate her. She is a reflection of the eternal light, a spotless mirror of God's activity, an image of his excellence. She is indeed more beautiful than the sun, surpasses all the constellations, and compared to light itself, she is more brilliant." — St. Maximilian Kolbe

$\mathcal{M}$aximilian was born in Poland. At the age of twelve he had a vision of the Blessed Mother. "I asked the Mother of God what was to become of me. Then she came to me holding two crowns, one white, the other red. She asked if I was willing to accept either of these crowns. The white one meant that I should persevere in purity, and the red that I should become a martyr. I said that I would accept them both."

At age sixteen, he joined the Conventual Franciscans, making his final vows on November 1, 1914. In 1917, while still in the seminary, Maximilian and six friends started the Immaculata Movement (*Militia Immaculatae,* Militia of Mary Immaculate) to advance devotion to the Blessed Mother as the path to Christ.

Maximilian was ordained in Rome on April 28, 1918, and received his Doctor of Theology on July 22, 1922. He returned to Poland to teach history at the seminary. To fight religious apathy, he started a magazine called *Knight of the Immaculate*. In 1927, he founded Niepokalanow, "the City of the Immaculate Conception," near Warsaw, with similar foundations in Japan and India.

ST. MAXIMILIAN KOLBE

In 1939, following the Nazi invasion of Poland, Maximilian was arrested. After a brief exile he and his brothers were released on December 8, 1939 (Feast of the Immaculate Conception), and the men returned to their publication work, including material that was considered anti-Nazi. Maximilian was arrested and imprisoned in Pawiak prison, Warsaw, Poland, on February 17, 1941.

On May 28, 1941, Maximilian was transferred to Auschwitz and branded as prisoner number 16670. He was assigned to a work group. At one point his guards beat him and left him for dead. At the camp hospital, he spent his time hearing confessions. Returned to the camp, Maximilian ministered to other prisoners, said Mass, and distributed Holy Communion.

Death-camp policy regarding escapes was that ten men were slaughtered in retribution for each escaped prisoner. In July 1941, there was an escape. When Francis Gajowniczek, a married man with young children, was chosen as one of the ten to die, Maximilian volunteered to take his place, fulfilling the destiny he chose when the Blessed Mother presented him the two crowns. Maximilian died at the death camp on August 14, 1941, by lethal injection after three weeks of painful starvation and dehydration. His body was burned in the ovens and his ashes scattered. The courageous priest was beatified on October 17, 1971, and canonized October 10, 1982.

Prayer to St. Maximilian Kolbe

Dear St. Maximilian Kolbe, you truly lived the gospel and a life of purity. You gave your life freely in response to God's grace, wearing the two crowns presented to you by the Blessed Mother. Please pray to the Blessed Trinity for me for the graces I need most. Ask the

Blessed Mother to intercede for me as I follow God's holy will in my life. St. Maximilian Kolbe, pray for us and for all who invoke your aid. If it is in God's holy will, please grant me (here mention your request). Amen.

24. St. Michael the Archangel

Feast Day: September 29 (with Archangels Gabriel and Raphael)

Patron of a holy death, the sick, sailors, emergency medical technicians, paramedics, knights, police officers, ambulance drivers, coopers, hatters, fencers, radiotherapists, artists, bakers; against temptation

"Now war arose in heaven, Michael and his angels fighting against the dragon; and the dragon and his angels fought, but they were defeated and there was no longer any place for them in heaven."
— REVELATION 12:7-8

St. Michael the Archangel is the leader of the army of God. From the time of the apostles, Michael has been invoked and honored as the protector of the Church. Scripture describes him as "one of the chief princes" and the leader of heaven's forces in their triumph over the powers of hell.

Opinions vary as to Michael's rank. St. Basil and other Greek Fathers placed him over all of the angels. Others believe he is the prince of the seraphim, the first of the nine angelic orders. According to St. Thomas, he is the prince of the last and lowest angelic order.

Muslims, Christians, and Jews all have devotions to Michael and writings about him. He is considered the guardian angel of the nation of Israel. Tradition tells us that Michael caused a medicinal spring to spout near the ancient city of Colossae. The sick who bathed there, invoking the Blessed Trinity and St. Michael, were cured. Other miracles have been attributed to him in association with various springs, and apparitions of the archangel have been observed in several locations over the centuries.

Christian tradition assigns four roles to St. Michael: 1) to fight Satan; 2) to rescue souls of the faithful from Satan's power, especially at the hour of death; 3) to serve as champion of God's people: the Jews under the old covenant, the Christians under the new; 4) to call souls away from the earth and bring them to judgment.

St. Michael is represented in art as an angelic warrior with full armor: helmet, sword, and shield. His shield often is marked with the Latin inscription *Quis ut Deus*, which has the same meaning as his name: "Who is like God?" Michael is usually

ST. MICHAEL THE ARCHANGEL

61

depicted standing over the dragon (which represents Satan), sometimes piercing it with his sword. He often holds a pair of scales, in which to weigh the souls of the departed, or the Book of Life, a symbol of his role in the Last Judgment.

Prayer to St. Michael the Archangel

St. Michael the Archangel, defend us in battle. Be our defense against the wickedness and snares of the devil. May God rebuke him, we humbly pray. And you, O prince of the heavenly host, by the power of God, thrust into hell Satan and the other evil spirits who prowl the world seeking the ruin of souls (from Pope Leo XIII).

St. Michael, protect us from evil and grant us (here mention your request), if it be God's holy will. Amen.

25. St. Monica

322-387 • Feast Day: August 27

Patroness of abuse victims, alcoholics, spouses in difficult marriages, widows, victims of verbal abuse, parents with disappointing children, victims of adultery, homemakers, wives, mothers

> *"Nothing is far from God."* — St. Monica

Monica was born in 322 in North Africa. Most of what we know about her comes to us through the writings of her son, St. Augustine of Hippo. Monica was a Christian from birth. Her spiritual director was St. Ambrose of Milan.

Monica was known for her gentleness and patience. Given in marriage to a bad-tempered and adulterous pagan, she suffered much. Still she prayed constantly for his conversion, and he finally converted on his deathbed.

Monica's son, Augustine, led a sinful life, fathered a baby out of wedlock, and joined the heretical Manichean cult. Upset that her son was ruining his life and could go to hell, Monica prayed unceasingly for him. She went to St. Ambrose and pleaded with him to persuade her son to leave the cult.

ST. MONICA

The bishop told her that she had nothing to worry about. "Go now, I beg you," he said, "It is not possible that the son of so many tears should perish." Monica continued pleading with God for her son's conversion and was delighted when her prayers were answered.

Augustine once recalled when his mother told him that she had lived her whole life to see him become a Catholic, so she was ready to die. A few days later, she was stricken with a high fever that proved fatal. On her deathbed she said, "Bury my body wherever you will; don't let care for it cause you any concern. One thing only I ask you, that you remember me at the altar of the Lord wherever you may be." She died shortly thereafter.

63

In the 1800s, a confraternity under the patronage of Monica was established to unite mothers in prayer for their husbands and children. Its rank quickly advanced to archconfraternity, and it spread all throughout the Catholic Church.

Prayer to St. Monica

Dear St. Monica, your devotion as a mother and wife and your commitment to your family, especially in your prayer for them, sets a powerful and timely example for us all. Please pray to the Blessed Trinity for me, my family, and all I hold dear so that we will be open to the graces that Our Lord in His great mercy wants to shed upon us. Help mothers and wives everywhere to know that Our Lord never turns His ear away from a mother's faithful prayers for her family. St. Monica, pray for us and for all who invoke your aid. If it is in God's holy will, please grant me (here mention your request). Amen.

26. St. Padre Pio

1887-1968 · Feast Day: September 23

Patron of civil defense volunteers

"Go ahead! Courage! In the spiritual life he who does not go forward goes backward. It is the same with a boat which must always go forward. If it stands still, the wind will blow it back."
— St. Padre Pio

Padre Pio was born in Pietrelcina, Italy, on May 25, 1887. Ordained a Capuchin priest on August 10, 1910, Padre Pio stayed home with his family for six years due to ill health. In September 1916, he was sent to the friary of San Giovanni Rotondo, where he remained until his death.

Pio was the first priest known to receive the stigmata, the visible wounds of the Cross. He bore these wounds for fifty years as he carried out his priestly ministry, inflamed with the love of Jesus. His Masses usually lasted one and a half to two hours, and in his teaching, he stressed the nature of the Mass as a holy sacrifice.

ST. PADRE PIO

Padre Pio was known as a great confessor, hearing confessions for ten to twelve hours a day. Millions came from all over the world seeking his counsel and consolation. He also possessed the gift of reading people's hearts. Pio's life can be summed up in three words: simplicity, humility, and obedience.

Unjust accusations led Rome to order Padre Pio to stop saying Mass in public and hearing confessions while he was investigated (1931-1933). Although it caused him suffering, he abided by the restrictions without bitterness, until the matter was resolved.

Padre Pio possessed a great love for the poor. He lived a life of great sacrifice and deep prayer. Demons sometimes tormented him, but he was close to the holy angels, calling upon them often for assistance and protection. He was never without a rosary and preached that the quickest way to heaven is "dear Mother Mary."

Word about Padre Pio's saintliness and supernatural gifts spread around the world. More than eight million people came to see him in his last years. On September 23, 1968, Pio voiced his last words, "Jesus, Mary," before breathing his last breath at the age of eighty-one. In the years following his death, miracles occurred around the world through his intercession as his reputation for sanctity continued to grow.

The friar was beatified on May 2, 1999, and then canonized on June 16, 2002. Many are comforted with St. Padre Pio's famous but simple statement: "Pray, trust, and don't worry."

Prayer to St. Padre Pio

Dear St. Padre Pio, you were an extraordinary servant of God, following in the footsteps of St. Francis of Assisi. In heaven you continue to serve God by interceding for us. Your heart went out to the poor. Help me to have eyes to see those in need around me and ears to hear the cries of the poor. Pray for me, please, that I may receive the graces I need to participate deeply in the Holy Sacrifice of the Mass. Please help me to desire humility, simplicity, and the spirit of obedience in my walk of life. Help me to realize the power in suffering united to the will of God. St. Padre Pio, pray for us and for all who invoke your aid. If it is in God's holy will, please grant me (here mention your request). Amen.

27. St. Patrick

389-461 • Feast Day: March 17

Patron of Ireland

> *"I am a debtor exceedingly to God, who granted me such great grace that many peoples through me should be regenerated to God and afterwards confirmed, and the clergy should everywhere be ordained from them for a people newly come to belief."*
> — St. Patrick

St. Patrick was born in the year 389. His birthplace is uncertain. At the age of sixteen he was taken as a captive to Ireland to serve a heathen master of herdsmen. He escaped to the Continent and was taught in the schools of Tours and Lerins, seeking education to be an instrument and apostle of God so that he would be able to convert Ireland.

Pope Celestine I commissioned him for the mission, and he received episcopal consecration in 442. He then began his missionary work to convert a pagan nation. The story of his use of a shamrock to explain the Trinity is still told today.

St. Patrick died on March 17, 493, in the monastery of Saul, in County Down, in Ulster. There, his remains and those of St. Bridget are buried in one grave.

Dear St. Patrick, you said, "I was like a stone lying in the deep mire; and he that is mighty came, and in his mercy lifted me up, and verily raised me aloft and placed me on top of the wall." Please pray that our dear Lord will also raise me up and heal my stony heart. You also said, "In a single day I have prayed as many as a hundred times, and in the night almost as often." Pray for me, dear St. Patrick, that I may have an increased desire to pray more deeply — to lift my heart often throughout the day in prayer no matter where I am and no matter what I am doing, so that I may fulfill God's holy will in my life. St. Patrick, pray for us and for all who invoke your aid. If it is in God's holy will, please grant me (here mention your request). Amen.

28. St. Peregrine

1260-1345 · Feast Day: May 1

Patron of the sick, especially cancer patients, AIDS sufferers, those with open sores, skin diseases, and breast cancer

> *"And great crowds came to him, bringing with them the lame, the maimed, the blind, the mute, and many others, and they put them at his feet, and he healed them."* — MATTHEW 15:30

Peregrine Lazoisi was born into a wealthy family in 1260 at Forli, Italy. He spent his youth in a worldly way. As a young man he became involved in politics and opposed the Church. One time when he was engaged in a dispute, he slapped the papal peace negotiator, St. Philip Benizi, across the face. St. Philip turned the other cheek and then prayed for the young man, and Peregrine converted.

Peregrine received a vision from the Blessed Mother. She instructed him to go to Siena, Italy, to join the Servites. He followed her instructions, received his formation, and was ordained. He was assigned to his hometown parish.

For thirty years, Peregrine worked in complete silence without ever sitting down — an act of penance for his earlier life of sin. When he did speak, he was an excellent preacher and a loving confessor. Eventually, he founded a Servite house in Forli.

Peregrine developed a growing cancer on his foot, which in time required an amputation. The night before the scheduled surgery, Peregrine prayed all night and received a vision of Jesus healing him with a touch of His hand. In the morning, Peregrine awoke to find his cancerous foot completely healed.

In 1335, Peregrine died of natural causes. His body is incorrupt.

St. Peregrine

69

He was beatified on September 11, 1702, and canonized on December 27, 1726.

Prayer to St. Peregrine

Dear St. Peregrine, you recognized your sinful past and attempted to make up for it while here on earth. Please pray for me to be able to discern what should be rooted out of my life and how I can come closer to God. Please ask Our Lord to heal (person's name) of cancer if it is His holy will. St. Peregrine, pray for us and for all who invoke your aid. If it is in God's holy will, please grant me (here mention your request). Amen.

29. St. Rita of Cascia

1386-1457 · Feast Day: May 22

Patroness of lost causes, the impossible, desperate cases, difficult marriages, widows, victims of physical spousal abuse, parents, the sick; against loneliness and sterility

> *"Blessed are the poor in spirit, for theirs is the kingdom of heaven."* — MATTHEW 5:3

Rita was born in 1386 in Umbria, Italy. She was drawn to holiness as a young child and visited the Augustinian nuns at Cascia often. At the age of twelve, Rita was betrothed to Paolo Mancini, a bad-tempered and abusive man. They were married when

Rita was eighteen, and she eventually gave birth to twin sons.

For eighteen years, Rita endured a difficult marriage, much abused by her husband. One day Paolo was stabbed to death. His sons sought revenge on their father's killers. Rita pleaded with them to forgive and refrain from violence. She stormed heaven with prayer, asking God to take their lives while they were in a state of grace so that they would not perish in hell. Her sons forgave the offenders shortly before their untimely deaths.

The call to religious life beckoned Rita now that she was alone. But some of the sisters at the Augustinian monastery were related to the assassins and denied her entry to religious life, fearing that Rita would cause trouble. Rita prayed to St. John the Baptist, St. Augustine of Hippo, and St. Nicholas of Tolentino for assistance, and at the age of thirty-six she was finally admitted to the monastery of St. Mary Magdalene.

Rita was a peacemaker and lived for forty years in the convent, praying and working for peace. She was devoted to Our Lord's Passion and asked Him if she could suffer as He had. She was blessed with a wound in her forehead, like a thorn from Christ's crown of thorns. The wound bled for fifteen years, and Rita lived with constant pain.

SHRINE OF ST. RITA OF CASCIA

Sickness confined Rita to bed rest for the last four years of her life. She ate little more than the Blessed Eucharist. When she was close to death, she was asked by a visitor if she wanted anything. She requested only a single rose from her family's garden in her hometown. The visitor went there in January, and in the dead of winter brought back the single rose that miraculously bloomed on an otherwise bare branch.

Prayer to St. Rita of Cascia

Dear St. Rita, Our Lord entrusted you with a portion of His Passion when He gave you the wound in your forehead from His crown of thorns. You bore your suffering in life, and the pain from the sacred wound, patiently and lovingly. You lived your life in great holiness, ushering your sons and husband to heaven. Please pray to the Blessed Trinity for me that I may be granted the graces that I need most. Please help me never to give up hope for any soul, continuing my prayers for those in need of salvation. St. Rita, pray for us and for all who invoke your aid. If it is in God's holy will, please grant me (here mention your request). Amen.

30. St. Teresa of Ávila

1515-1582 • Feast Day: October 15

Doctor of the Church; patroness of headache sufferers, lace-makers, the sick, members of religious orders

> *"You ought to make every effort to free yourselves even from venial sin, and to do what is most perfect."*
> — St. Teresa of Ávila

Teresa was born on March 28, 1515, in Ávila, Spain. When she was only twelve, her mother died. The young girl threw herself before a statue of the Blessed Virgin and asked her to be her mother.

Teresa's father put her in a convent at age sixteen to straighten her out. Eventually, she learned to love the convent and felt that it was a safe place for a person such as herself who, she felt, was prone to sin.

Teresa was granted many favors by God. Sometimes she levitated while in prayer. She experienced visions and heard voices. At first, all this troubled her, but her spiritual adviser convinced her that the visions and locutions came from God.

Explaining the concept of mental prayer, Teresa once said, "For mental prayer in my opinion is nothing else than an intimate sharing between friends; it means taking time frequently to be alone with him who we know loves us. The important thing is not to think much but to love much, and so do that which best stirs you to love. Love is not great delight but desire to please God in everything."

When Teresa was forty-three, she sought to found a new convent that would go back to a simple, reverent life. She had a special love for St. Joseph and said that he had never failed to aid her in all her necessities. Because of this, she called the new convent St. Joseph's, which was devoted to the enclosed spiritual life rather than the more relaxed style of the time.

She established other convents based on the strict rule followed at St. Joseph's. When she started her second convent, she met a young friar, John Yepes (John of the Cross). Teresa founded her first monastery for men at Duruelo in 1568 and then turned it over to John. She traveled all over Spain reforming the Carmelites, while writing about her life. Pope Gregory XIII recognized the Discalced Reform, as it was called, as a separate province of the order. Teresa's letters and books are now widely regarded as classics of spiritual literature. Among the best known are her *Autobiography*, *The Way of Perfection*, and *Interior Castle*.

ST. TERESA OF ÁVILA, FROM A VATICAN STATUE

Teresa died October 4, 1582 (October 14 by the Gregorian calendar, which went into effect the next day and advanced the calendar ten days). Thirty-two monasteries of the Reformed Rule had been established by that time; seventeen were convents for nuns.

Teresa was declared a Doctor of the Church on September 27, 1970, for her writing and teaching on prayer. She was the first woman to be honored in this way.

Prayer to St. Teresa of Ávila

Dear St. Teresa, you were a persistent and feisty woman. I pray that I can emulate your virtues and persevere in prayer to act upon what God is calling me to do in my life. Please teach me to pray with my heart, loving Our Lord, seeking His holy will unconditionally. Help me to remain positive as you did and to continue to move forward on the narrow path. Please ask your friend, St. Joseph, to help me in my life, too. St. Teresa, pray for us and for all who invoke your aid. If it is in God's holy will, please grant me (here mention your request). Amen.

31. St. Thérèse of Lisieux

1873-1897 • Feast Day: October 1

Doctor of the Church; co-patron of the missions with St. Francis Xavier

"You cannot be half a saint. You must be a whole saint or no saint at all." — ST. THÉRÈSE

Marie Françoise Martin was born at Alencon, France, on January 2, 1873, the youngest of nine children of Louis Martin, a watchmaker, and Zelie Guerin. Zelie died when Marie was only five. The family moved to Lisieux, where Marie was raised by her older sisters and her aunt.

Two of Marie's older sisters became Carmelite nuns, and Marie wanted to follow in their footsteps. She was refused at first. But later she was admitted to the Carmel of Lisieux and professed in 1890, when she took the name Thérèse of the Child Jesus.

SHRINE OF
ST. THÉRÈSE OF LISIEUX

Thérèse suffered from tuberculosis, which she bore patiently. She was convinced of the power of prayer, saying, "My whole strength lies in prayer and sacrifice; these are my invincible arms; they can move hearts far better than words. I know it by experience."

She served for a time as mistress of novices at the convent. In 1894, she was asked by the prioress, Mother Agnes (her sister Pauline), to write the story of her childhood. In 1897, with her writing completed, the new prioress, Mother Marie de Gonzague, ordered her next to tell about her life in the convent. Both stories were combined in *Story of a Soul*, which became a popular modern spiritual autobiography.

Thérèse died on September 30, 1897, when she was only twenty-four years old. She quickly attracted a following of devotees, who considered her to be "the Little Flower" and "the Saint of the Little Way." Thérèse was beatified April 29, 1923, and canonized in 1925. She was declared a Doctor of the Church as well as co-patron of the missions, with St. Francis Xavier. In 1944, she was named co-patroness of France with St. Joan of Arc.

Prayer to St. Thérèse of Lisieux

Dear St. Thérèse, I admire your holy life and your faithfulness to your state of life, as you wanted only to please Jesus. You have said, "For me, prayer means launching out of the heart toward God; a cry of grateful love from the crest of joy or trough of despair: it is a vast, supernatural force that opens out of my heart, and binds me close to Jesus." Please help me to see prayer as a means to come closer to God; help me to "launch" my heart to Him through joy and despair. You remind us that we should "miss no single opportunity of making some small sacrifice, here by a smiling look, there by a kindly word; always doing the smallest thing right and doing it all for love." Help me remember that nothing is small in the eyes of God, and that all of the little things we do in love become huge in His eyes. St. Thérèse, you have promised, "After my death I will let fall a shower of roses." Please shower them upon me. St. Thérèse, pray for us and for all who invoke your aid. If it is in God's holy will, please grant me (here mention your request). Amen.

32. St. Thomas More

1478-1535 · Feast Day: June 22

Patron of lawyers, widowers, large families, those with difficult marriages, adopted children, court clerks, statesmen, civil servants, politicians

> "I will not mistrust him . . . though I shall feel myself weakening and on the verge of being overcome with fear. I shall remember how St. Peter at a blast of wind began to sink because of his lack of faith, and I shall do as he did: call upon Christ and pray to him for help. And then I trust he shall place his holy hand on me and in the stormy seas hold me up from drowning." — ST. THOMAS MORE,
> IN A LETTER FROM PRISON TO HIS DAUGHTER

Thomas was born in 1478 in London. He studied law and became a page for the archbishop of Canterbury before embarking on a legal career that took him to Parliament. Thomas married Jane Colt and became a devoted family man, the father of one son and three daughters. His wife Jane died at a young age, and Thomas then married Alice Middleton.

Thomas was a friend of King Henry VIII. He was Lord Chancellor of England, a position that was second only to the king. Thomas resigned the chancellorship in 1532 at the height of his career. He and his friend St. John Fisher refused to recognize the king as the head of the Church of England. He also could not agree with Henry on the matter of the king's divorce.

Thomas spent the remainder of his life writing in defense of the Church. He was imprisoned in the Tower of London because he refused to compromise his religious beliefs to suit the king's political demands. Fifteen months later, St. John Fisher was executed, and nine days afterward, Thomas was tried and convicted of treason.

He told his judges that he hoped they "may yet hereafter in heaven merrily all meet together to everlasting salvation." On the scaffold, he told the crowd of spectators that he was dying as "the king's good servant, but God's first." Thomas was beheaded on July 6, 1535. He was canonized in 1935. Some of his best-known writings are his *Treatise on the Blessed Sacrament* and *Utopia*.

St. Thomas's head is kept in the Roper Vault at St. Dunstan's Church in Canterbury, England. His body is at St. Peter ad Vincula, in the Tower of London.

Prayer to St. Thomas More

Dear St. Thomas More, you never compromised your faith, even when opposed by the king. Teach me to be faithful at all times to the one true King. You prayed, "Give me the grace to long for your holy sacraments, and especially to rejoice in the presence of your Body, sweet Savior Christ, in the holy Sacrament of the altar." Please pray that my faith will increase as well as my love for the holy Mass and the Blessed Sacrament. St. Thomas More, pray for us and for all who invoke your aid. If it is in God's holy will, please grant me (here mention your request). Amen.

About the Author

DONNA-MARIE COOPER O'BOYLE, a Catholic wife and mother of five, and a Lay Missionary of Charity, has received awards for her work and apostolic blessings from Pope Benedict XVI and Pope John Paul II. She was chosen by the Pontifical Council for the Laity to attend an International Women's Congress in Rome.

Donna-Marie is the author of the best-selling book *Catholic Prayer Book for Mothers* (Our Sunday Visitor, 2005), *The Heart of Motherhood: Finding Holiness in the Catholic Home* (Crossroad, 2006), and *Prayerfully Expecting: A Nine Month Novena for Mothers-To-Be* (Crossroad, 2007), which bears a foreword by Blessed Teresa of Calcutta. Donna-Marie's books were endorsed by Blessed Teresa of Calcutta and blessed by Pope John Paul II.

Donna-Marie's work can be seen in Catholic magazines, newspapers, and on the Internet. She has a regular radio segment on Ave Maria Radio. Donna-Marie can be reached at her website, www.donnacooperoboyle.com. She provides daily inspiration at her blogs: "Embracing Motherhood" at www.donnamarieembracingmotherhood.blogspot.com and "Daily Donna-Marie" at www.donnamariecooperoboyle.blogspot.com.